BASE
PAIRS

Maria
Melendez

Acknowledgments:
A few poems in this collection have previously appeared in *Perihelion, Organization & Environment,* and *ISLE.*

I wish to thank my little family, my writing sisters, and the Putah-Cache band of merry pranksters for all their support and inspiration. Gracias and abrazos to Sandra McPherson, Gary Snyder and Steve Culberson for helping bring these poems to their current life.

Swan Scythe Press

Department of English
University of California, Davis
One Shields Avenue
Davis, CA 95616

Editor: Sandra McPherson
Associate Editor: Steve Culberson
Cover Design: Mark Deamer
Book Design: Maria Melendez
Cover Art: Carlos Licon, by permission of Carmel Castillo

Base Pairs/Maria Melendez
ISBN: 1-930454-12-0

© 2001 by Maria Melendez

All rights reserved. This book or parts thereof, including artwork, may not be reproduced in any form or by any means, electronic or mechanical, including photocopying, recording, or any information or storage retrieval system now known or to be invented, without written permission from the author, with the exception of brief quotations embodied in critical articles or reviews.

Contents

I: Matter ≡ Anti-Matter

The Bothered-by-Questions Method	6
The Unformed Heart	9
In Biruté's Camp	11
Sensing Home: Fluvial	12
Why Not Attempt the Summit	13
Assaying the Source	16
One-Minute Wail	19
An Illustrated Guide to Things Unseen	21
Smoking Topos	23

II: Matter ≡ Matter

Visitation	26
I Preferred to Unearth Angelica Root	28
Spring Green Just a Dream Locked in Aspen Bark	30
A Different Sympathy	31
Arborphilia Pantoum	32
Recombinations	33
Sensing Home: Aural	34
A Decent Swim	36
Epilogue: Poeta Falsa	37
Notes	40

I. Matter ≡ Anti-Matter

❧ THE BOTHERED-BY-QUESTIONS METHOD

"How do you tell the difference?" "Lunate scar within the ligule
                                        signals Great Basin witchgrass."
(The new-moon birthmark on his underarm—)
                                              "Am I prying?"

"Run some gels (color-coded chromosomes pulled apart like slip-faults)
    to see if these ryegrasses are related."
                                             This is the new day.

                "First, we admitted our search for knowledge
                was beyond our control."

Beyond dispute, without a doubt, sure, see "certain,"
see how each pair of answers
breeds unknowns.

                      "Second, we loaded a car with ecologists
                      swapping rhino stories
                      and drove to the interrogation pen
                      (a square of earth with chicken wire
                      to exclude deer from our study)."

How to tell them apart: "A mule deer's ears and face make a Y
                as it peers over the hilltop at ecologists on all fours
                        with stubby, seedling ears."

Oh, so harsh! The scientists have no say in their phenotypes...
"Have you ever heard a rhinoceros fart? I mean WHOA.
Blow, Gabriel!"
                                              This is the new day.

"If we could exclude the foghorn and seals barking,
we'd do that too—we're required by custom to isolate single factors."

                                        "not custom or lecture, not even the best,"
"To study the effects of seal calls on coast grass,
we'd have to grow two sets of grass in sound-proof cases and
                                                            pipe in a 'bark'

                              "not words, not music or rhyme I want,"

every one-point-three minutes, to say nothing on the effects
                                      of varying 'bark' frequencies— "

                      "only the lull, the hum of your valved voice"

                                   Anything to say...
about cold fusion?
"Cold fusion? Yes, I drink it for breakfast every morning!"
                                                    Love those nuclei...

Fourth, we made a "fearless and searching inventory"
of Bodega Reserve's insedimentors:
    wire flags marking study boundaries,
    ninety centimeter PVC pipes,
    roots of coyote brush,
    shells washed up or harvested, smashed;

"Can I eat this can I eat this can I eat this this this what about this?"
                versus
        "Show us what to eat."

"Does this belong does it belong where do I or this does this belong
                                       here here or here?"
    versus
  "Show us what is here."

                "...depends on what the definition of 'is' is."

"A weed is there for a reason;
it's healing the land or it's the only thing that can grow there."
                                              You are the new day.

  The best days of hunting deer or hunting knowledge follow
nights of sleeping with black sage
    crammed beneath your armpits to hide your scent

hide your scent, spray your pencils and data sheets with eau d'vole,
aim your questions up from under the ground (such as,
                                  "The ground hides a fault,
    so then why this apparent perfection and balance above...
    Is it because of my faulty iris?").
Unless you want your questions to be droppings that fall from your
                                                  mouth
(a perfectly respectable gesture) to mark your turf—

Mix confusion into your coffee at the start of every day...
                                        And you are these questions.

Trippers and askers, trippers and askers,
    "Earth possesses words that never fail."
(And can't be mined or yoursed...)
                                                  We are in question.

❧   THE UNFORMED HEART

Ask her if she regrets anything.

I was
daydreaming tiny serpents—
I worked in a lab.
We magnify events
when there are questions.
We probe the source data.

Ask her how he touched her.

I never wondered why.
It all seemed natural.

Ask her how he touched her.

His voice swung to me
like a rope ladder.

Ask her what she remembers.

There were always oak leaves
stuck to my skirt.
I felt we were unbuilding each other.

An addictive molecular fit
when he stood near,
some near-combustive cellular groan:

> *oh, you again—*
> *aren't we beautiful?*

Chromosomes became
divided adders
swimming to their poles
and I refused.

This made us closer,
like shared deformity.

Ask her if drowning hurts.

We'd fallen through so many lifetimes
to hear blue oaks commanding us
to kiss.

Ask her if drowning hurts.

Unlike spawning,
    I went inland
for the procedure.
Outside, a crow was panting in the ash tree.

You expect to search forever for a soul mate
through a world submerged in surprise.

Suppose you actually meet—

                  the ungodly consequences.

Do you regret this love?

    Long before I was touched, we were fused.

    It was the fault
    of the planet.
    Even blue oaks slip
        toward extinction,
    perched high on their primary need
        when water is far below.

IN BIRUTÉ'S CAMP

Suppose God is looking for a good
 piece, who could be you with that bare
  strip of scalp parting your long hair,
 braided loose and looped up in the swamp heat,
sweat curling around your small, bristly eyebrows,
 your hands gleaming with juice and pulp
  as you hammer fruit on the feeding platform.

 That strange orangutan,
the human-raised one called Pan-gan,
 who throws men off the dock
  like an overzealous baptizer, may
 be a god and here he comes
  padding side to side onto your platform in the swamp.
 If he curves the ridiculous length of his
tendon-riddled arms around your waist
and wrestles you down to the wooden boards,
  scream—he'sbitingyouhe'stryingtokillyou—no,
he's pushing up your skirt—

   become limp below the waist and make your torso
 a flexible branch for him to squeeze
  as he swivels from one world to the next;
 (now he is calm and deliberate,

    now his eyes roll upward)

  When he finally moves off
   the feeding platform and into the trees,
    rise into this loss, which is relief:
  his seed will shimmer out of you, unrecognized.

❧ Sensing Home: Fluvial

Who would've thought heartbreak sounded like water running through the pipes of a Texas "waterman," curving like a big metal staple out of the ground, who would have thought heartbreak had a swirl and whoosh, a multi-octave spill and *plink plink* underscored by bass rhythms *tungung*; ancient water pumped up from no-one-is-sure where, city sucking long drags off a source that could give out any day (without prayer). Patches of my skin where cell layers should be wavy and elastic have flattened out and become thin, and my soul and I can barely speak to each other. She's moved back to the coastal hills and this is all the fault of the dammed fork of Putah, plugged at both ends: if all of us lived within earshot of flowing water, if wave-action were allowed to purl our dreams, my skin would know the arc of health, and that dense air which my skin loves most would have a deep serenity that the pull of current brings. Steelhead trout, lamprey, and seasoned abalone stories need to spawn inland, I call for more canoeing! Is it only the splash of wine in a glass that gives me this impression—a slight rustle in the deergrass where no one has found a fawn in years? A Hmong man hung himself in my apartment building last year, unable to scrape the algal residue of dreams from his eyes each morning; it is the nature of water to meander and to flood, no one survives this place. O Putahtoi, what movement, what fierce, bed-bursting motion!

Why Not Attempt the Summit
Mount Shasta City, 1999

All night the buried mouths
   beneath our condos lecture us,
      we can hear their blather
  extrude up into fir trees,
the diminishing clinks of words
   chiming minor keys
      on their way to the stars.
Love as much as you
can, don't throw your heart
*   away to just one god, wash*
      the baby in mint, watch
where you step on the mountain,
things that live so high
  don't want visitors.
      Feed them whiskey, concrete,
   cigarette or bone ash, doesn't matter,
nothing keeps them shut.
   So we trust their advice and vow,
      with our red and recycled breath,
   never to scramble or crawl above
the porous wall of trees
   that mark a crooked timberline
      along the gravel and scree.
   We'll only go far as the limber pines,
and won't presume to chase spirits
   over tinkling shales.
      We mind this limbed boundary
   because the town mechanic
crossed over it in a vision
   that almost killed him; andesite grains
      winked up at him from the highest slopes,
   and he dove into their dark fission

of mineral and glass;
   but when the valley drew his stone limbs down,
      the gravitational tow
of his hoard of sleeping relatives
nearly tore apart
   his breath from bones, from heart;
      he tumbled out of the dream
in a surge of scalding rock and scarlet vapors.
We don't tempt this verge
   because andesite is not a visionary's word,
      snow-wet andesite is
metamorphic and too-visionary,
and the tiny pink blooms
   of alpine Campanula (which deeply
      thinks to grow an inch
each quarter century) would snare us
into slow, endless worship—
   our children would go hungry.
      (We know these perennials
   from stories that the dirt dreams up—)
We keep to our side of the trees
   because the firs themselves are near enough
      to provide sufficient comfort
to subsist on, and so much
has already sloughed
   from the sure face of the land for us,
      and to learn the grace
   in songs to praise the spiders
living that high, we'd have to die
   or want to die and ever after hope
      for nothing else but death.
   Because the need to be self-referential

every instant above treeline
   is lethally disorienting to us:
       always having to look at one's
   trunk to be assured of one's existence,
to look at oneself and not one's surroundings
   to verify what one is.
       In the alpine, only the winged
   know who they are in reference
to shifting slopes; we're not shaped
   to rise and flow on updrafts.
       We live behind the scar
   of this limit because there are no houses,
of devotion or otherwise, above
   the timber; because we were created
       in the firs' image and remain,
   like the firs, unclassifiable;
we try to prefer
   forest enclosure to Krumholz exposure
       because we need to ask for nothing
   from at least one space because great powers,
wild and hunted,
   sought and supplicated to,
       need a place to be left to themselves,
   to their own devices.
Pleading erodes creators
   under any circumstance,
       and there are no perfect worshipers
   for these gods outside all measures of perfection.
They need a high, storm-cleansed
   refuge, sparkling with silence,
       to perch and preen on when valley air
   becomes polluted by exhausted ghosts.

ASSAYING THE SOURCE

Anyone can declare themselves a shaman
in these mutable days.
How did their supposed powers choose them?

    Have they pounded death
        on a stone and licked
        its juices? Made death a topical
        ointment or an enema?

        I, the poet of recombinant blood,
            half   manzanita   half   mestiza
        I declare that colors come loose
            from the night
        and swarm my palms.
        I profess language to be byproduct
        of the wheatgrass
        disarticulating August.

But any ribald poet or other biotechnologic
engineer
can declare herself well-trained and worthy

    to aim plastic pipets
        at the ribosomal Author
        of life, squirt out demands
        for significant info;

        Nora, my life-long Wonder Twin,
            (whose arms are soft as mullein),
        dares to still the universe
            of cells
        by freezing DNA under a microscope.
        Yes, the Great Work is healing,
        and she may help
        beat lymphoma.

But expertise begins when you get wind of
how to revivify
your own bones. Can you practice without poison?

    Not the putrefaction
        of "connecting with"
        your inner poisons, but the Poison
        Path, where "fungi" and "flora"

                allies offer all the lessons of the New World
                      (sacred science, molecular vision)
                to any who'll learn helpful rhythms for eating
                          knowledge,
                to any whom they don't kill first. Physical therapists
                say Nora's chronic hip pain comes from too much
                sitting, studying how to snap genes apart
                like Bristle Blocks.

    It's easy to forget to praise your poisons: with supposed perfectability of
    progeny and prosody, the source of corrupt life and mutant language
    hardly seems worth thanking.

And anyone can declare themselves
creator
in these days that glance off edges like a clumsy hammer.

    Give us more cell phones
        so our radiating voices can
        jar the beaks of passing gulls,
        and coagulate within each other's organs.

    Give us more phone lines
        to the cell, give us more
        cruelty-free cosmetics,
        more guilt-free, sacrifice-free colors.

Let's sell make-up as sacred paint,
        (give us Avon in the Amazon!),
Let's make it all up as we go along.
        Nora,
reassure me: when you descend the twisted ladder
into dreams, do intertwined snakes nearly
crush you between them as they tell you what you're doing
is both deadly and permitted?

❧ ONE-MINUTE WAIL
(Just Add Carbaryl!)

This valley never spawned a religion of emptiness, not with Early Girls
lining the causeway like lice from the backs of elephant trucks.

Put in sheep to barber the bushy tomatoes,
recover some losses after the plant has closed.

Kids always sympathetic to the wind, opening windows
on the school bus to let it in like a beggar.

I was born in the blurry mind of the desert in rain, came here to take
                                                    my place among
rows of olive trees, old scholars lined up at a urinal.

(Who cares if words are emptiness, they motor things along
like a thin, strong muskrat tail.)

(Who cares if they are tiny compared to the tendrillar galaxy,
we still love the oak gall that grows
its delicate shell and inky dust around the peewee wasp.)

Swerving through a storm of corn debris, I'd like to tip my head and
                                                                  drink up
all the yellow duster has to offer.

You know that once-popular Italian way
of painting love: a young man with hands chained
around a tree?
That is not what I mean—
maybe it's closer to the lusty crow who,
if you are the only man left, will jump you
with a cloacal kiss to collect a genesis.

I'll give back to these crows and crops and chemicals,
I'll add my own carbonic praises (mono or di-oxide,
                depends on if I walk or drive) to the mix.

Heavy-lidded bucks are watching out for us from between the branches.
Just as crushed buckeye powder stuns fish for harvest, so will
                                            crop dust stun us
and we'll float up on our backs to flat, blue heaven and wait for a meal.

An Illustrated Guide to Things Unseen

Here's the turquoise cheek
of a fathead minnow,
netted from the camo-tint
    can't-ever-see-what's-in-it-creek
    dropped on your palm, it's glowing lilac thread
    of spine bisects what—is?—your lifeline.

        Here's the spirit of a rhododendron garden
           (slurp slurp slurp, it's all for show)
        impersonating "Redwood Grove" in an arboretum.

Here: two pipevine swallowtails
    crazy with the indigo smell of each other,
spiraling past a grinning red cat
    in the ivy, past a bearded man
        on a picnic bench who's leaving
        a short-haired woman, here's
        anger fastening over her
        like an acorn cap.

Here's a rapist's habitat
between snowberry bushes
and live oak shadows.

           Here's a whole night
heron rookery in a cottonwood,
and here's a woman feeding stuffing
to the ducks; she has bitten the tip
of her baby's little finger.

Here, the reburied bones
of the first woman exhumed during
construction of a Performing Arts center—

            Here's a poisonous oleander
            concealing a well (and not so well,
                                    after all)
            from hypothetical polluter-
                        terrorists.

For those of you suffering from
absence of riverflow,

      here's bowlegged Waterman
            stuck in the ground ("vacuum breaker");
    within his corroded metal,
      swish and rattle of water tumble,

                unlappable; its curling rhythm
          mimics the undercurrent of silence
        in the waterway you're trying to love,
            the unyielding laminar surface
            that's breaking your heart.

꩜ SMOKING TOPOS

Cautionary contour lines are not for preserving the soul
of land or "the solace of open spaces"; the purpose behind a topo map
is for me to know my land better than my enemy;
hide missiles, take cover—
I wish for a picture of topos untainted
by nervous intention. But isn't a white tobacco flower,
blossoming on surveyed land, a signal
of the same nerves? I wish for a pure cigarette:
no formaldehyde (that's for frogs, foetal pigs and brains
    and the little dissected shark on my desk in Field Biology, old Carlson
    pacing the rows with his salt-and-piss smelling flannel,
    his tranquil snort on a backpacking trip when I flew off a cliff
    and into a cold Tuolumne swimming hole shouting ffffuuuuuuuuck,
    my jealous best friend shoved me when I crawled out shivering,
    what, I said, what? It ain't no big thing, as the guy I used to make
                out with in boxcar-sized newspaper bins
used to say; the way I knew he wasn't real was that only the headlines
came all over me, bits of words smudged my hands and belly.
This imaginary boy said "no big thing" about sneaking out nights
                                  to shoot deer
    in the blue gum woods of the VA Hospital—close range, with a
                                    pistol.
    Don't know if he ever killed any; by the time he'd even mention
                                  the deer,
I'd be too ground into the funnies to care. He was the most
                                  bewitching
    of the now exhausted shade lovers, polluted by my
    calling up too much, without hacking off
    any offerings or penance) no spongy filter
no cyanide twizzling out the end no Virginiaboro bowling alley
                                  image
to contend with, something to take a long drag off and then pucker

back out, something to help me see the concentric contours
of my wind so I can know those exhaled buttes and gullies
better than any enemy, and can see that breath is real in fantasy—
I'll keep muttering on to stay informed of coulees to hunch in,
creeks to jump in, with cuss-words for parachutes.

II. Matter ≡ Matter

VISITATION

God save the amateurs

and their faith that something gorgeous
as a comet tumbles toward us
from outside the tidy orbit
we have known;

that some white-hot, divine refrain,
like an arpeggio of epochs,
will reverberate across
our fertile nights.

When Hale and Bopp grew tipsy
with the frenzy of their numbers
showing, *Brightest one in human
history,*

something must have started smiling
as it felt them both projecting
and attracting jagged bolts
of lightning hope.

When I moaned through my night labor,
its bright head and heat-flung tail
beaded a blessing on my forehead,
and I pushed,

straining to show another shocker
through the cold hospital window,
and the glass fogged up with breath
on either side.

After the mash and sear of pain,
labia swollen to the size
of some magnificently bruised
magenta fruit,

with a small, burst vein streaking red
across my eye, time spread, open and warm
for the release
of this one, smooth skein.

But the thirty-four hundred years
between our species and the comet now
are dripping down like icicles
at noon;

yes I should look to my son,
inhale the amber from his scalp,
but he, alone, is just too small
to re-direct

the coming flood of generations.
I'm afraid to ask the question:
Who
will still fit the random orbit
of Surprise?

I Preferred to Unearth Angelica Root

The breath of deer
grazing across the disappearing
surfaces of dusk

would wake him if I
laid him, sleeping now, between
the sagebrush.

Eight weeks after moon's dilation
into full glare,
midwife says I look tired, meaning

crescent shadows cup my eyes.
Fine, I say during house call, oh, I'm fine;
then I tell the purple hollow of a lupine

how, in the daze of dailiness,
I want to leave this baby
laid out for the coyotes to decide:
                          protect, feed on, ignore.

Husband is afraid of my quadrupled breasts,
their lipid-rich excess
that rivers down my flannel shirts;

geometry is the only thing to love
about nursing, the satisfaction of arcs
bending into each other:

baby forehead rounded in profile
into nose and cheek to breast to "c"
of small, open mouth;

feeding unites only by shape—
his frantic heart still beats on its own,
against all other impulses;

I preferred to unearth Angelica root,
or a blade of creeping wildrye,
but instead, I had a boy.

SPRING GREEN JUST A DREAM
LOCKED IN ASPEN BARK

Back muscles still clenched
from the recent expulsion of life,
still living I trudge up the trail to our home.

Each lumbering step
spans a galaxy cluttered
with pebbles, mud and clumps of slush.

Three bee-sized snowflakes
clutch the blanket that covers my son,
heavy with sleep in my arms.

> A sandhill crane's breath
> in corrugated song
> rolls out through the valley—
>
> or two
> beginning a nest
> by weaving their voices
> through firs, aspen, the ice on the river,
> through weasels, mice, a child and his mother—
>
>> or each sliver of air has arisen
>> as a single, rattling call.

And look—the entire darkening valley
showered by thousands of soft, white flowers.

A Different Sympathy

                If the cord snared
your raw vagina when you pulled
your purple newborn up
to nurse, and every suck was cat-
tongue, nipple smashed, demanding
milk you couldn't make yet
and no one told you, "It's all right,
you will become numb as polished stones,
flow with life," then two days later,
veins in your breasts turned hot-iron hard
and the magmatic flood of your milk
drenched all your clothes, stank up your room,
stained your bed, and no one told you,
"It's all right, this roar of pain
will soon recede into a trickle,"

  and if, on a slow walk,

you saw the river's bulging edge,
   where waters gouge troughs
       with loyal licking,
where a cow moose's tracks
   yield up in grainy swirls
       and dissolve,
then you, too, would hunt for reeds,
   weave a tiny boat; humming low
       old songs, you'd push your son
   to root on the breast
       of the river.

ARBORPHILIA PANTOUM

The shock of seeing you standing alone
    (in the brittle grasses) manzanita,
        reaches of red bark thin and smooth as throat skin—
the closer I walk, the more your color divides,
    manzanita in brittle grass;
        (touching you feels like touching my baby son)
    the closer I walk, the more deep red dissolves
        into orange, black, and yellow, streaming through,
            like touching the skin of my baby son
        when we can't get enough of each other,
(yellow, black, orange, getting enough of you—)
        he'll squeeze my breasts in the bath, shriek, "Mama!,"
when we can't get enough of each other—
he'll grab my face with butterfly hands,
    poke for the corner of my eye, "Mama eyes!,"
        as I rub soap on his round little tummy;
he'll grin, hold my face in butterfly hands,
        grope with his feet for the slope of my belly
    as I hold him, rub soap on his round little tummy.
Who is it I'm stroking, my hand on this branch,
        remembering feet on the slope of my belly
            as your red arms grope the paths of my brain;
    who is it I'm stroking, my hand on this branch,
        and what will my fingers have taught you,
            with your red arms forking into my brain—
the spark of desire arcs out of my palms, into your veins,
        and will my fingers at least have taught you
            the seeping oil of my skin, rooted child —
the spark of desire arcs out of my palms, into your veins,
        reaches of red bark thin and smooth as throat skin;
            loneliness oils my bones, rooted child,
        at the shock of seeing you standing alone.

🌀 RECOMBINATIONS

       Expectation: Reality:

to be needed by the world,
and by Solano grass, a rare
(rare=endangered=fragile=dependent)
Central Valley plant, delicate and lovely.
            Solano grass: the plant world's wet mutt:
            clumpy, drooping leaves, pale inflorescence
            rising in a spike of tiny, ragged glumes,
            pointed at the tip which, my naturalist's
            curiosity revealed, tasted like battery acid.
      The patch of Tuctoria offered up its
      strongest inner oils, anticipating
      my warm, animal tongue.

Mexican chocolate=
a source of Chicana revelation=
Aztec holy music singing up the palate.
            First, dark cup was good, gritty,
            but no ancestral voices in sweet steam.
      Tia Luz sang "The King of Glory Comes"
      while stirring in the Oaxacan chunks,
      and the kitchen macaw squawked along.

Love, when finally bound in gold=
compassion big across as the valley,
wholeness pure as sleep.
            Love enacted daily: a Formica table top
            stained with Tension Tamer tea,
            a renegade worm of last week's spaghetti
            crusted underneath.
      Our first table, bought at Goodwill,
      had little gold strands painted into it,
      extra leaves to make it longer
      for our children.

🐚 SENSING HOME: AURAL

A beautiful long-nosed Japanese guy came in from the coast range to attend the inland university, traveled to my classroom (built over Patwin burials) along the Pomo-Patwin trade route called I-80. Shells for money harvested by Pomo, carried inland where the coins were minted by Patwin here in Putahtoi. *You know my coins are counterfeit, the anadromous moneys just re-shaped homes of ocean creatures....you know my coins are counterfeit, but you accept them anyway, my impudence and my pretending...*that I was his teacher, like saying it's the hanged who kills the noose. The day he pulled me into the ocean was a day without prayer and therefore the kind of day that can give out from under you like green glass—the instant you start to wonder if it's water because some punk student put the idea in your head, then you're down, eyes open on the bottom, can't see nothing. (Somebody could be bluffing.) A feathery mud rises up between your fingers as you press the bed, or had you been swimming down here all along?...Walking the glass wasn't a dream, more a story you closed your eyes and spun around yourself like a cocoon, some shape in which to dissolve, then poke your head out of to find fluid all around...I'm not trying to say that a man led me to the ocean and instructed me on the dos and don'ts of abalone diving while a strange iridescence curled, wave after wave, around his lips... I'm saying a wave opened its mouth—a young man leaned forward in his chair and something happened to the air that pocketed his shoulders so that I couldn't breathe, a man put his head on his desk and looked up through half-closed eyes shaped like one-sided coins (a shape with one side and a shape with infinite depth are easily mistaken for each other) and told me about his father night-diving for outlawed harvests, about how white people pound the shit out of abalone, how Japanese know to never run heat through that meat....all that happened was a man demanded some attention and next thing I know my feet are floating above my head and I'm reaching down at 45 degrees, not even remembering I have lungs, reaching and kicking down for the luster under calcified shell, reaching for the meat of the animal's foot.... Then he went on, voice deep as a foot-drum, to tell me he wanted a farm and twenty ugly kids, oh, I love that, I burbled. What noise, what beautiful noise, the coins clattering against each other in a leather pouch, the tinkle of chimes outside the window where my toddler whimpered through nights when I was weaning him to paw-print spotted cups of (slightly toxic) tap water....What beautiful whispered promises between shell and polishing cloth—currency for acorn mush or a bride, from such shellfish come the morning giggles and nighttime chuffling snores of children, O Putahtoi, such sounds, such braided, endless waves!

A Decent Swim

> Hoes Down Harvest Festival
> Capay Valley, CA

You can't blame me for not skinny dipping
when it felt like my uncles from Arizona, New Mexico,
LA and San Diego were all there,
silver-buckle belly and big cowboy hat
almost wide as shoulders, crisp western shirt:
the Ranchero band taking a break, scuffing dirt
in a loose circle by the creek could've been
Tios Raul, Antonio and Oscar poking fun at each other,
pretending not to notice pale breasts and
behinds spanked by afternoon sun.

No one told me that as I watched my toddler son and husband
wade out together like two distant ships
I was sitting on the best gravel in the world,
my aggregate fears clinging like clothes
that should have come off.

Young men undressed next to me, their bodies
slid in the water and settled like mercury.

We'd all walked down a jungle of salt cedar
to get to the banks of Cache.

Peeling off my sweaty socks, I waded in to find my family,
and let the creek reclaim the spaces between my toes.

🌀 POETA FALSA

Students in my public writing workshops often ask me, "How do you write a poem?" I panic, because I don't know! Mostly I feel like a big phony in front of these classes. Here, with some inspiration from Michelle Serros' Chicana Falsa, *is why:*

The truth is, I'd sooner show you my quaint
    endeavors, than read aloud
        this squishy, spiritual
            condensation.
Don't get much from Lowell or Bishop,
    though I do like
      (say it)
      like Joy Harjo.
If my mouth is open and I'm yammering on
    about pushing your inner editor aside
            don't
trust me—
    I'm not writing.
Don't let me tell you
    the pen in your hand
    is a fully sanctioned inner-child play activity;
when I pick up my worn-out toddler
from 8 hours of day care, I wonder again—
      couldn't my time have been better
    spent?
Anytime I'm waving a teacherly pom-pom,
    (The Mystery! The Mystery! Fun! Fun! Fun!)
  I'm not on the field, and any old day
I'm just someone who wishes she could write a poem,
    or someone who doesn't give a rip
  about poetry at all. (Isn't that Zen of me?
            All that non-attachment?)
    Only while I'm writing, that top plate of
      my skull having dissolved
        under the fluorescent heat

of night herons in live oaks,
                the rhythmic tremble
        of all our chain-linked DNA,
when I'm extruding through the cracks
                in all that hum,
only then could someone say,
        oh yes, she knows
                the crows' throaty chirps, knows
                        imagination pours into a vacuum,
or poetry seeks its own level and spills from not there
                into there until it's half-way heard.
Why writing?
        Because construction workers' clank and clatter can't go
                                                unanswered,
        Because there isn't even a breath's partition between worlds,
        Because at no other time do I feel as penstemon-like, red,
                                                bizarre and open—
        Because at no other time am I as half-assed and ragged
                                                as the early draft,
                or as mammoth,
            as orchestral, as the near-end.

NOTES

The **Base Pairs** are adenine=thymine and guanine≡cytosine.

Matter and **Anti-Matter:** See David Robertson's *Real Matter* and Putah & Cache poster #14.

The Bothered-by-Questions Method: This poem owes a few lines to Walt Whitman and President Clinton, and contains real and imagined quotations from two ecologists who graciously let me tag along on their field work, Kevin Rice and Eric Knapp.

The Unformed Heart: after Louise Glück.

In Biruté's Camp: In her book, *Return to Eden*, Biruté Galdikas, a prominent researcher of orangutan ecology, documents the rape of one of her camp assistants by a male ex-captive orangutan named Gundul.

Sensing Home: "Putahtoi" is Patwin for Putah homeplace.

Why Not Attempt the Summit: "A friend said to me, 'When civilization has finally ended, what will you miss the most?' I said, 'The tinkling of ice cubes in a glass.'" Gary Snyder

Assaying the Source: Thank you to Inés Hernández-Avila for the term "sacred science."

I Preferred to Unearth Angelica Root: "I would like to give birth to things like endangered species and not humans."
    Sandra McPherson, in an interview with Bill Moyers

COLOPHON

This chapbook is set in Adobe Jenson, designed for digital composition in the new millenium by Robert Slimbach. Adobe Jenson combines the strength and beauty of a pair of Renaissance type icons, Nicolas Jenson's roman and Ludovico degli Arrighi's italic typeface. Printed on warm white 70# Sundance Vellum (50% recycled, 30% post-consumer) at The Printer in Davis, CA.